...κ Water

John
HUNT
Publishing

ISBN 1 85608 241 5

Write to: John Hunt Publishing, 46a West Street,
New Alresford, Hants SO24 9AU

The rights of Mark Water and Sue Climpson to be
identified as author and illustrator of this work have been
asserted by them in accordance with the Copyright,
Designs and Patents Act 1988

A CIP catalogue record for this book is available
from the British Library

Manufactured in Singapore

INTRODUCTION

Travel today is big business. The whole world is opening up to the tourist. Remote mountain villages, vast untouched beaches, hidden cities are packaged now and sold to anyone — anyone with a bit of money that is!

There are serious travellers, adventurous travellers like Colombus, Scott, Marco Polo, Abraham; and there are those who journey within:

gurus, priests, poets and thinkers. They have been there. They can help us on our way, comfort, guide and enlighten, in meeting, leaving and parting.

The Lord your God goes with you; he will never leave you nor forsake you.

THE BIBLE,
DEUTERONOMY 31:6

The longest journey
is the journey within.

DAG HAMMARSKJOLD,
1905-1961

He who keeps one end in view

makes all things serve.

ROBERT BROWNING,
1812-1889

Go placidly amid the noise and the haste, and remember what peace there may be in silence.

MAX EHRMANN

*A good person is always a novice
in the ways of the world.*

MARCUS MARTIAL,
40-140

Be strong and courageous.
Do not be terrified; do not be
discouraged, for the Lord your God
will be with you wherever you go.

THE BIBLE, JOSHUA,
JOSHUA 1:9

When we have wandered all our ways, Shut up the story of our days. And from which earth, and grave, and dust, The Lord shall raise me up, I trust.

Sir Walter Raleigh, 1552-1618,
WRITTEN ON THE EVE OF HIS EXECUTION

He that travels far

knows much.

CLARK,
1639

He [God] knoweth the way

that I take.

THE BIBLE,
JOB 23:10 AV

Hurry is not of the devil,

hurry is the devil.

JUNG,
1875-1961

In the middle of the trackless universe, Jesus Christ is the way.

SELWYN HUGHES,
TWENTIETH CENTURY

He rides at ease whom the

grace of God carries.

THOMAS A KEMPIS,
1379-1471

To travel hopefully is a better thing than to arrive.

ROBERT LOUIS STEVENSON, 1850-1894,
Virginibus Puerisque, El Dorado

Let no worldly cares make you
forget the concerns of your soul.

BISHOP THOMAS WILSON,
1663-1755

People wish to be settled: only as far as they are unsettled is there any hope for them.

R.W. EMERSON,
1803-1882

All travelling becomes dull in exact proportion to its rapidity.

JOHN RUSKIN,
1819-1900

The eternal God is your refuge,

and underneath are the

everlasting arms.

THE BIBLE, MOSES,
DEUTERONOMY 33:27

The fool wanders,

the wise man travels.

FULLER, 1732

The way to do is to be.

LAO TZU, 600 BC

Truth may walk through the world unarmed.

BEDOUIN PROVERB

*Happiness is the harvest
of a quiet eye.*

AUSTIN O'MALLEY

*Here I am! I stand at the door
and knock. If anyone hears my
voice and opens the door,
I will come in and eat with him,
and he with me.*

THE BIBLE,
REVELATION, 3:20

Lead, kindly light,
amid the encircling gloom,
Lead thou me on...

...The night is dark, and I am far from home; Lead thou me on...

...Keep thou my feet; I do not ask to see The distant scene: one step enough for me.

JOHN HENRY NEWMAN,
1801-1890

Oh! for a closer walk with God,

A calm and heavenly frame;

A light to shine upon the road

That leads me to the Lamb!

WILLIAM COWPER,
1731-1800

We are in the Father,

And we are encircled in the Son,

And we are encircled in

the Holy Spirit...

...And the Father is encircled in us, And the Son is encircled in us, And the Holy Spirit is encircled in us. Allmightiness, All Wisdom, All Goodness, One God, One Lord.

JULIAN OF NORWICH,
1342-1416

Blessed are those whose strength is in you, who have set their hearts on pilgrimage.

BIBLE,
PSALM 85:5

*Our heavenly Father never takes
anything from his children unless
he means to give them
something better.*

GEORGE MULLER,
1805-1898

Our God is a strong tower.

MARTIN LUTHER, 1483-1546,
AFTER THE BIBLE, PSALM 144:2

The best of all is,
God is with us. Farewell.

DYING WORDS OF JOHN WESLEY,
1703-1791

Lives of great men all remind us

We can make our lives sublime,

And, departing, leave behind us

Footprints on the sands of time.

HENRY WADSWORTH LONGFELLOW,
1807-1882, A PSALM OF LIFE

I will go anywhere
provided it is forward.

MOTTO OF DAVID LIVINGSTON,
1813-1873

Do not worry about your life...Look at the birds of the air;...your heavenly Father feeds them. Are you not much more valuable than they?

THE BIBLE, JESUS CHRIST,
MATTHEW 6:25-26

Christ with me, Christ within me
Christ behind me, Christ before
me, Christ beside me, Christ to
win me, Christ to comfort
and restore me.

ST PATRICK'S BREASTPLATE, 375–466,
ADAPTED BY ALEXANDER

Christ beneath me, Christ above me. Christ in quiet, Christ in danger, Christ in hearts of all that love me, Christ in mouth of friend and stranger.

ST PATRICK'S BREASTPLATE, 375-466, ADAPTED BY ALEXANDER

I am satisfied that when the Almighty wants me to do or not to do any particular things, he finds a way of letting me know it.

ABRAHAM LINCOLN,
1809-1865

In all the things thoughout the world, the men who look for the crooked will see the crooked, and the men who look for the straight will see the straight.

JOHN RUSKIN,
1819-1900

I will instruct you and teach you

in the way you should go;

I will counsel you and

watch over you.

THE BIBLE,
PSALM 32:8

*A*nd I said to the man who stood

at the gate of the year. 'Give me a

light that I may tread safely into

the unknown.'...

...*And he replied, 'Go out into the darkness and put your hand into the Hand of God. That shall be to you better than light and safer than a known way.'*

M. LOUISE HASKINS

This is how men get to know God – by doing his will.

HENRY DRUMMOND,
1851-1897

*Go confidently in the direction
of your dreams! Live the life
you've imagined.*

HENRY DAVID THOREAU,
1817-1862

I bind unto myself today
The power of God to hold and lead,
His eye to watch, His might to
stay, His ear to harken
to my need...

...The wisdom of my God to teach, His hand to guide, His shield to ward, The word of God to give me speech, His heavenly host to be my guard.

ST PATRICK
375-466

Let nothing disturb you, let nothing frighten you: everything passes away except God; God alone is sufficient.

TERESA OF AVILA,
1515-1582

Dear Lord, of Thee three things I

pray: To know Thee more clearly,

Love Thee more dearly,

Follow Thee more nearly

Day by day.

RICHARD OF CHICHESTER,
1198-1253

Where can I go from your Spirit?

Where can I flee from

your presence?...

THE BIBLE,
PSALM 139:7

...If I go up to the heavens, you are there; if I make my bed in the depths, you are there.

THE BIBLE,
PSALM 139:8

Put on the full armor of God so that you can take your stand against the devil's schemes.

THE BIBLE,
EPHESIANS 6:11

Tomorrow has two handles:
the handle of fear and the handle
of faith. You can take hold of it
by either handle.

UNKNOWN

The Lord will keep you from all harm – he will watch over your life...

THE BIBLE,
PSALM 121:7

...the Lord will watch over your coming and going both now and forevermore.

THE BIBLE,
PSALM 121:8

Keep your heart in peace; let nothing in this world disturb it: everything has an end.

JOHN OF THE CROSS,
1542-1591

Those who seek God in isolation from their fellow men,...are apt to find, not God, but a devil whose countenance bears an embarrassing resemblance to their own.

R.H. TAWNEY,
1880-1962

*Teach us, Lord, to serve you as
you deserve, to give and not to
count the cost, to fight and
not to heed the wounds...*

*...to toil and not to seek for rest,
to labour and not to ask for any
reward save that of knowing that
we do your will.*

IGNATIUS LOYOLA,
1491-1536

Do not think it wasted time to
submit yourself to any influence
which may bring upon you
any noble feeling.

J. RUSKIN,
1819-1900

Forgetting what is behind and straining forward to what is ahead, I press on towards the goal to win the prize for which God has called me heavenward in Christ Jesus.

THE BIBLE,
PHILIPPIANS 3:13-14

God be with you till we meet again; When life's perils thick confound you, Put his arm unfailing round you: God be with you till we meet again.

J.E. RANKIN,
1828-1904

Wherever he may guide me,
No want shall turn me back;
My shepherd is beside me,
And nothing can I lack.

A.L. WARING,
1820-1910

Lift up your heart to him, sometimes even at your meals, and when you are in company: the least little remembrance will always be acceptable to him. You need not cry very loud; he is nearer than we are aware of.

BROTHER LAWRENCE,
1611-1691

Lead us on our journey,
Be thyself the way
Through terrestrial darkness
To celestial day.

G.R PRYNNE,
1818-1903

In my Father's house are many rooms... I am going there to prepare a place for you.

THE BIBLE, JESUS CHRIST,
JOHN 14:2

Fear God, and where you go men
will think they walk in
hallowed cathedrals.

R.W. EMERSON,
1803-1882

In simple trust like theirs who

heard, Beside the Syrian sea,

The gracious calling of the Lord,

Let us, like them, without a word

Rise up and follow thee.

J.G. WHITTIER,
1809-1892

*Enrich, Lord, heart, mouth,
hands in me, With faith, with
hope, with charity: That I may
run, rise, rest with thee.*

GEORGE HERBERT,
1593-1633

May the road rise to meet you,

may the wind be always at your

back, may the sun shine

warm on your face...

...and rain fall softly on your

fields; and until we meet again,

may God hold you in the

hollow *palm of his hand.*

GAELIC BLESSING

My Presence will go with you,

and I will give you rest.

THE BIBLE,
EXODUS 33:14

*J*esus Christ is the same yesterday
and today and forever.

THE BIBLE,
HEBREWS 13:8

*Praise ye and bless ye the Lord
and give thanks unto him: and
serve him with great humility.
Alleluya, alleluya!*

FRANCIS OF ASSISI, 1181-1226,
TRANSLATED BY MATTHEW ARNOLD

Though we travel the world over to find the beautiful we must carry it with us or we find it not.

R.W. EMERSON,
1803-1882

Let us have faith that right makes might; and in that faith let us to the end, dare to do our duty as we understand it.

ABRAHAM LINCOLN,
1809-1865

*Still to the lowly soul He doth
himself impart, And for his
dwelling and his throne
Chooseth the pure in heart.*

JOHN KEBLE,
1792-1866

Lord, we thy presence seek;

May ours this blessing be:

Give us a pure and lowly heart,

A temple meet for thee.

JOHN KEBLE,
1792-1866

I know not where his islands lift
their fronded palms in air;
I only know I cannot drift
Beyond his love and care.

J.G. WHITTIER,
1807-1892

Trust in the Lord with all your

heart and lean not to your

own understanding...

THE BIBLE,
PROVERBS 3:5

...in all your ways acknowledge him, and he will make your paths straight.

THE BIBLE,
PROVERBS 3:6

Lord Jesus,

I give you my hands to

do your work.

I give you my feet to go your way...

...*I* *give you my eyes to see as you do. I give you my tongue to speak your words. I give you my mind that you may think in me...*

...I give you my spirit that you may pray in me. Above all, I give you my heart that you may love in me your Father and all mankind...

...I give you my whole self that you may grow in me, so that it is you, Lord Jesus, Who live and work and pray in me.

THE GRAIL PRAYER

Where can I go from your Spirit? If I rise on the wings of the dawn, if I settle on the far side of the sea, even there your hand will guide me.

THE BIBLE,
PSALM 139:7,9,10

I am with you always,
to the very end of the age.

THE BIBLE, JESUS CHRIST,
MATTHEW 28:20